COUNTERTRADE
Business
Practices
for Today's
World Market

Leo G. B. Welt

AMA Management Briefing

AMA MEMBERSHIP PUBLICATIONS DIVISION
AMERICAN MANAGEMENT ASSOCIATIONS

D0874771

Library of Congress Cataloging in Publication Data

Welt, Leo G. B.
  Countertrade.

  (AMA management briefing)
  Bibliography: p.
  1. Countertrade.   I. Title.   II. Series.
  HF1412.W44 1982   658.8'48   82-18443
  ISBN 0-8144-2285-3

American Management Associations, New York.
All rights reserved. Printed in the United States of America.

Second Printing

About the Author

Leo G. B. Welt is president of Welt Barter and Countertrade, a division of Welt International, a Washington, D.C.-based firm that assists and represents U.S. companies in their overseas business, particularly in Eastern Europe, the Soviet Union, and China.

Mr. Welt is publisher of a number of international newsletters, including *China Business & Trade, East/West Technology Digest, Latin American Index, Soviet Business & Trade* and *Washington Report on Africa.* He is the coauthor and editor of two business guidebooks: *Information Peking* and *Information Lagos.* Articles by Mr. Welt have appeared in many newspapers and magazines such as the *New York Times,* the *Washington Post* and *Business America.*

A native of Berlin, Mr. Welt's first experience in barter was trading the family china for food in postwar Germany. He was educated in Berlin and in the United States, graduating from Princeton University in 1958. Prior to establishing Welt International Corp. in 1967, he conducted international trade in management positions for International Paper, Weyerhauser Company, and Miehle-Goss Dexter. In 1975, Welt International became the first company to receive the president's "E

Award" for exports to East European countries.

Mr. Welt is an active member of the President's Export Council and a number of regional trade associations.

Contents

1

The Growing Importance of Countertrade in International Commerce

When businessmen speak of countertrade, they often describe the practice in its simplest terms—trade without money. Although this definition distinguishes countertrade from strictly cash-for-goods transactions, it fails to convey the variety and complexity of this method of trade as it appears today.

Countertrade encompasses any commercial arrangement in which purchases are made to offset sales as a means to reduce or restrict the flow of scarce hard currency across national boundaries. Although this includes such practices as evidence accounts and clearing arrangements, reciprocal sales and counterpurchase arrangements are the more common forms of countertrade.

Historically, countertrade has been associated with East-West trade. Now, as a result of many developing countries' shortage of convertible currency, the pressure for countertrade has been mounting in trade involving Third World states. This study focuses on the general experience of Western firms doing business using countertrade, primarily with the East Bloc and with developing countries.

REASONS FOR IMPOSING
COUNTERTRADE OBLIGATIONS

1. *To Preserve Hard Currency*—Countries with nonconvertible
   currencies look to countertrade as a way of guaranteeing
   that expenditures of hard currency for foreign imports are
   offset by hard currency earnings generated by the foreign
   party's obligation to purchase domestic goods.
2. *To Improve Balance of Trade*—Nations whose exports to the
   West have not kept pace with imports and who are concerned with both the reality and appearance of trade deficits,
   increasingly rely on countertrade as a means to balance
   bilateral trade ledgers.
3. *To Gain Access to New Markets*—As a nonmarket or developing country increases its production of exportable goods,
   it often does not have a sophisticated marketing channel to
   sell the goods to the West for hard currency. By imposing
   countertrade demands, foreign trade organizations utilize
   the marketing organizations and expertise of Western companies to market their goods for them.
4. *To Upgrade Manufacturing Capabilities*—By entering com-

The conditions and terms of countertrade arrangements can vary
greatly from case to case. Some countries, Romania and Indonesia, for
example, have general countertrade requirements set out in their laws
governing foreign trade. Most countries, however, impose countertrade demands depending on the specific characteristics of the transaction being negotiated. Some have internal directives, others leave it
to the domestic organizations. Bear in mind that all the actors a
Western businessman may encounter when he negotiates a foreign sale
may not have the same interests.

The countertrade obligation that arises in the course of negotiations
is usually a percentage of the value of the sale, ranging from a small

pensation arrangements, under which foreign (usually Western) firms provide plant and equipment and buy back resultant products, the trade organizations of LDCs (less developed countries) can enlist Western technical cooperation in upgrading industrial facilities.

5. *To Maintain Prices of Export Goods*—Countertrade can be used as a means to dispose of goods at prices that the market would not bear under cash-for-goods terms. Although the Western seller absorbs the added cost by inflating the price of the original sale, the nominal price of the counterpurchased goods is maintained, and the seller need not concede what the value of the goods would be in the world supply and demand market. Conversely, if the world price for a commodity is artificially high, such as the price for crude oil, a country could barter its oil for Western goods (e.g., weapons) so that the real "price" the Western partner was paying was below the world price. (In this way a country could attract customers by means of a lower price than is officially available from OPEC countries without officially violating price guidelines, since the value of the imported goods would never be stated in monetary terms.)

portion to 100 percent or greater. Not only does the value of the countertrade arrangement vary, but the complexity of the transaction can span the spectrum from a simple barter deal, for instance, pig iron for oil, to complicated switches of credit among three or more different nations.

Only in rare instances today is countertrade actually conducted without the exchange of money. To use the analogy of farmers trading their goods, pure barter ("I'll trade you one pig for 20 bushels of corn") is not widely practiced. International countertrade today is more likely to involve a sales transaction ("I'll buy a pig from you for $20, but only if you agree to buy $10 worth of corn from me") or a variation of this

WESTERN MOTIVATIONS FOR PARTICIPATION IN COUNTERTRADE

1. *To Take Advantage of Sales Opportunities*—in order to make a sale in the markets of the nonmarket and developing world, it is often necessary to concede to countertrade demands. A company that is willing to engage in counter-trade may gain a competitive edge over one that is not.
2. *To Gain a Source of Supply*—in some cases, particularly in compensation transactions, countertrade can be used by a Western company to obtain a long-term, reliable supply of raw materials, component parts, or finished products that may be inexpensive because of decreased labor costs and lower transportation expenses.
3. *To Gain Prominence in New Markets*—Western companies sometimes employ countertrade as a way to show good faith in certain markets, and to establish themselves as a reliable

involving the buy-back of the resultant product ("I'll buy a pig from you for $20, but only if you agree to buy $30 worth of pork from me when I slaughter the animal").

International countertrade is a sort of balancing act. By making certain that a foreign purchase is offset, at least partially, by a foreign sale, a buyer of Western technology, goods, or services can limit the depletion of hard currency on a transaction and limit the damage to his country's balance-of-payments position.

For these reasons and others (discussed later), developing and nonmarket countries* have found it attractive to impose countertrade obligations on Western imports as a short-term solution to hard-currency deficits. Western companies, however, are generally less enthu-siastic about this complicated and risky form of business. In addition to

*The term "nonmarket countries" refers to the European members of the Council of Mutual Economic Assistance (CMEA): Bulgaria, Czechoslovakia, East Germany, Hungary, Poland, Romania and the Soviet Union.

trading partner. By displaying a willingness to purchase domestically produced goods from a country, a Western firm may enhance its opportunities to gain major sales there in the future.

4. *To Adjust Their Accounting Record and Take Advantage of Tax and Tariff Laws*—for example, if the "true" market value of a countertrade deal is $10 million, both parties involved could understate the nominal worth of the transaction to $8 million. This means that less money has to be paid in tariffs or taxes by one or both parties (if the foreign partner is privately owned). This occurs often in compensation deals where a multinational exports parts to a foreign plant for assembly and understates the value of the shipment to avoid paying a higher tariff. The final price of the product then will overstate the value added during the assembly process. This is more easily accomplished with differentiated goods as opposed to raw materials or chemicals.

the inherent difficulties of negotiating, drafting contracts, financing, risk management, and—in some instances—disposing of the counterpurchased goods, Western firms are hesitant to purchase goods that are different from (or inferior to) those they would ordinarily deal in. Furthermore, the goods obtained by the Western companies often have inflated prices. In other cases, the goods obtained possess prices lower than market value, and may saturate and disrupt Western markets. Nevertheless, Western businessmen are overcoming their distaste for countertrade simply because they cannot afford to ignore the enormous markets in which this mode of trade has become a fact of life.

THE PREVALENCE OF COUNTERTRADE

Only a few years ago, international businessmen, particularly those in the United States, considered countertrade to be a primitive and archaic way of doing business. Today, according to the London *Economist*, countertrade represents about one-quarter of the world's $2.13 trillion of international commerce.[1] Of trade between the industralized West and nonmarket countries, about 50 percent is tied to some form of countertrade. With the availability of hard currency likely to decrease in the near term, the importance of countertrade is likely to grow.

Part of this increase is due to the cyclical tendency of countertrade to flourish during periods of world economic stagnation and to diminish during times of economic growth. When the economies of the industrialized world are healthy, nonmarket and developing countries are likely to have greater success in marketing their products for hard currency, while at the same time, Western companies are in a stronger position to refuse countertrade terms.

REASONS FOR ENGAGING IN COUNTERTRADE

The developing and nonmarket countries impose countertrade obligations for similar reasons. (See the box on pages 8 and 9 for summary.) Although Western companies generally prefer straight cash tranactions that are simpler and involve fewer risks, they have been willing to concede the countertrade demands. (See the box on pages 10 and 11.) The conditions under which certain countries demand countertrade are such that companies that are unwilling to do business in this form will find themselves excluded from an increasingly growing area of international trade.

2

Forms of Countertrade

Businessmen approaching the subject of countertrade may find the terminology somewhat bewildering. Part of this confusion stems from the lack of standardization in the vocabulary used. For example, there is no agreement on a single term for the practice of "countertrade" as a whole. Elsewhere, one may find "barter" or "compensation" used as a generic term to refer to the general practice referred to here as "countertrade."

Perhaps the greatest reason for this absence of uniformity is the relative newness of the particular types of countertrade now most widely in use. "Compensation," for instance, entered the field's vocabulary at the end of the 1960s. Similarly, "counterpurchase" (although it is closely related to older forms of countertrade) had not been practiced under its current contractual arrangements until fairly recently. As a result, economic organizations have lacked the data needed to arrive at precise and comprehensive terms and definitions.

This problem of definition is exacerbated by the fact that countertrade transactions are formed according to the contingencies of commercial conditions surrounding each individual deal. A barter transaction, for instance, may have elements of counterpurchase or compensation in it. A single trade transaction may also employ two or more forms of countertrade at once.

Another more particular reason for differences in terminology is that Eastern and Western parties in a transaction often choose to refer to a practice by different names. This is partially due to the difference in economic contexts of the two, but it is sometimes an intentional decision to emphasize one or another aspect of a practice.

VARIABLES IN COUNTERTRADE PRACTICES

Before beginning to define and discuss the various types of countertrade, it may be useful to examine a few of the characteristics by which countertrade practices are categorized:

Relative Duration—a countertrade transaction may take place within a matter of days, or may span a number of years.

Form of Settlement—hard currency may change hands, or only goods may be exchanged (pure barter).

Relation of Countertraded Products—in some cases, counterdeliveries are in the form of products resulting from the original sale (compensation); in others, products exchanged are unrelated (counterpurchasing).

Legal Arrangements—the countertrade transaction may occur under a single contract, or under two or more legal instruments.

Value Relations of Deliveries—counterdeliveries, as a proportion of original sale, range between a small percentage to well over 100 percent.

Size of Deal—countertrade practices are used for transactions involving sums as small as a few thousand dollars or as large as several billion dollars.

Technology Transfer Motive—countertrade arrangements are sometimes employed by a nonmarket or developing nation to acquire technology and, in other cases, consumer goods, agricultural commodities, or other products.

In the following definitions and explanations, the terms used are those employed most commonly by current authoritative sources.

Many individual transactions will fall into one category or another without embodying all of that form's characteristics, or one deal may incorporate more than one of the forms in a single commercial arrangement. By applying these definitions, however, one can identify the general variables of countertrade practice. For further clarification of the various forms of countertrade, see the Appendix.

BARTER

In recent years, pure barter—the exchange of goods under a single contract—has become rare, but not extinct. Barter is used most commonly today between nonmarket countries and poor developing countries, although Western companies occasionally involve themselves when the circumstance arises that a Western firm and the trade organization of a less developed country (LDC) or a Council of Mutual Economic Assistance (CMEA) country have roughly equal values of goods that they desire from each other at the same time.

Problems such as determining and agreeing upon the relative value of traded goods discourage interest in barter transactions. Another crucial disincentive is the use of one contract to cover both deliveries and counterdeliveries. Western banks are rarely willing to finance or guarantee a transaction in which a creditor's proceeds are contingent upon another party's performance. Moreover, even if guarantees can be obtained from a willing financial institution, the complexity of covering contingency risks in a barter contract with guarantees is a disincentive in itself.

There are no letters of credit in barter transactions, but participants may obtain parallel bank guarantees in the form of standby letters of credit or performance bonds. These ensure that, in the case of default, the defaulting party would compensate the performing party in hard currency. In most cases, however, it is easier simply to employ two separate contracts: one for the delivery and one for the counterdelivery of goods, and to have each party pay for the goods in hard currency with payment guaranteed by a letter of credit. This type of transaction is referred to as *parallel barter* or, more commonly, *counterpurchase*.[2]

COUNTERPURCHASE

Under a counterpurchase agreement, a Western company sells goods to a foreign trade organization in a communist or developing nation and contractually agrees to make reciprocal purchases from that organization, or from another commercial body in the same country, within a designated period of time. Counterdeliveries in these transactions are generally not resultant products (they are not produced by, derived from, or related to Western goods delivered in the original sale), but are chosen from among a range of products offered by the purchaser in the first contract. The duration of the entire transaction is relatively short—from one to three years, and the commitment for reciprocal purchase, stated in currency as a percentage of the original sale, varies from 10 percent to 100 percent, but is generally less than the full value of the original sale.

Counterpurchase is conducted under two separate contracts which may be linked by a protocol. Its financing can be organized in a fashion similar to that of standard trade, since each of the agreements is an exchange of goods for hard currency. Separating the contracts protects the original seller because payment for his goods cannot be legally withheld if problems arise in the execution of the second contract.

Unlike the first contract, which is a standard cash-for-goods agreement, the second contract is broader and more complex. Although it may call for the purchase of specific goods for a set price, usually it identifies a list of goods that may be chosen for purchase and the criteria for pricing rather than actual prices for the goods.

In East-West trade, it is often stipulated that reciprocal orders must be placed with the foreign trade organization (FTC) or, in China, with the foreign trade corporation (FTC) to which the original sale was made. In developing countries, the procedures vary. In many cases, however, goods may also be purchased from trade organizations other than that to which the sale had been made, or in the case of developing countries, from a different company. This practice of one entity purchasing the Western company's product and another providing the "counterpurchased material" is called "linkage."

Since counterpurchase is a short-term commercial arrangement for the exchange of goods, it does not typically involve significant technology transfer. Rather it is often employed by an Eastern or developing nation to acquire goods for which hard currency would not be otherwise allocated. In the case of CMEA countries, these are often products that are not included in the five- or ten-year plan, or hold a low priority in the plan. The amount of counterpurchase demanded on a sale is in inverse proportion to the importance of the good to the buyer's country.

Goods offered by East Bloc countries may be raw materials, manufactured goods, semimanufactured goods, machinery, and so on, but typically and increasingly they take the form of finished manufactured products. These are the products that have limited access to hard currency markets, often because of a lack of demand or low quality. Countertrade with developing countries in some respects resembles that with the nonmarket world, but the Western company is more likely to receive raw materials or oil in exchange for its products.

Normally, a counterpurchase agreement allows the seller in the first contract to assign his counterpurchase obligation to a third party—a trading house or other foreign buyer. If the Western company can find no products for counterdelivery that it can use in its own operations or that it can market through its organization, it often transfers its obligation to a trading house, which will dispose of the goods for a commission or "discount." These discounts range from under 5 percent for disposal of easily marketed goods such as raw materials, to as much as 40 percent for hard-to-market manufactured goods.

COMPENSATION

Compensation, often also called *buy back*, involves the sale of technology, equipment, or a plant with a contractual commitment on the part of the seller to purchase a certain quantity of products that are produced by or derived from the original sale. Because these transactions involve setting up entire production facilities, their values can run into hundreds of million of dollars. The duration of the transaction, accordingly, is far more lengthy than for counterpurchase arrangements owing not only to the magnitude of the projects, but also to the time necessary to complete projects before they come on stream to produce goods for counterdelivery. At a minimum, the period of the buy-back obligation runs 3 to 4 years, and it is not uncommon for a compensation arrangement to last 25 years or longer.

The commitment to buy back goods, as a proportion of the original sale, is also typically greater than for counterpurchase, with counterdeliveries often totaling 100 percent or more of the value of the original sale.

As in counterpurchase arrangements, compensation is conducted with the use of two separate contracts that may be linked by protocol.* The separation of legal instruments for deliveries and counterdeliveries serves the same function as in counterpurchase, but both contracts gain added importance both because of the need to keep large payments for the transfer of technology and goods unencumbered, and because the innumerable variables and contingencies inherent in the establishment of full-scale facilities places an added risk in the second, buy-back contract of a deal. Similarly, the protocol that links the two contracts in a compensation deal takes on greater importance by ensuring that counterdeliveries are, in fact, produced with the technology and equipment delivered in the original sale.

Unlike counterpurchase, it is the first contract in compensation that is more complex and poses more problems. The Western seller in the deal is often setting up a potential competitor, and in the contract to transfer technology and equipment, he must pay special attention to clauses pertaining to the second party's right to transfer technology, its right to use the Western company's brand name, and its right to distribute in certain market territories. These considerations make compensation negotiations a complex business, often taking a number of years to complete.

Nevertheless, compensation is the fastest growing form of countertrade in terms of dollar value. The Organization for Economic Cooperation and Development (OECD) has estimated that the value of compensation deals in East-West trade could be as high as $30 to $35 billion for the years 1969-1979, with Soviet and Polish deals accounting for the greatest share. The use of compensation in major projects did not emerge until 1969, when it was employed by metallurgical firms of

---

*It is useful to note that under the old definition, "compensation" was "buy back" under a single contract.

Austria and the Federal Republic of Germany to sell large-diameter steel pipes to the Soviet Union in exchange for subsequent deliveries of natural gas. It was not until 1974, however, that compensation began to flourish in East-West trade. In that year, according to the OECD, more compensation agreements were concluded by the Soviet Union and other CMEA nations than in all previous years combined.

These deals, referred to in the East as "industrial cooperation," are particularly attractive to the Soviet Union and other Eastern European nations because they involve a long-term participation on the part of the Western company. Through this long-term relationship, the Eastern party can obtain the technology, training, and capital goods by which to achieve their highest priority industrial projects, and to finance these projects, often entirely, by guaranteed exports to the West. China, in its recent modernization drive, has begun to place great emphasis on compensation for the same reasons, and the rest of the developing world may be expected increasingly to seek these arrangements as they aspire to obtain technology and capital imports for which they cannot afford to pay with hard currency.

Despite the complexity and risks, Western companies commit themselves to compensation agreements, particularly in these times of slack industrial development in the West, as a way to secure major plant, equipment, or licensing sales. In some cases, compensation can also offer guaranteed long-term supplies of energy products, raw materials, or manufactured goods that may be difficult to obtain and essential to the company's operation elsewhere. Manufactured goods may be less expensive in a compensation arrangement because of lower labor costs in a developing or communist country.

Additional profit may also accrue to the Western participant from sales that are not a part of the compensation deal itself, but are closely related to the deal. It is common, for instance, for the purchaser in a compensation arrangement to satisfy its needs for the product that will finally be produced by a compensation project from the Western participant until the purchaser can produce it himself. Similarly, it sometimes occurs that domestic demand for the products of a compensation project is greater than the projected surplus production after meeting counterdelivery commitments. In these cases, it is natural that the non-Western participant obtain the products from the Western party in the compensation deal, often under hard currency terms.

Compensation may greatly distort markets in specific products. If the trend continues with East Bloc and certain developing countries to provide semimanufactured and manufactured goods under buy-back arrangements with Western firms, the result may be saturation of particular markets. The Western company might dispose of its items in a particular market, while the technology that it has provided has led to increased production, which is also being marketed in the same country.

This sort of disruption has already occurred in some chemical markets of Western Europe. The petrochemical industries of West Germany, France, and Britain have been plagued in recent years by a flood of buy-back imports and dumped products produced in excess of East European needs—particularly bulk chemicals. Western European chemical equipment companies were happy to concede to compensation for major sales while their industry was facing hard times in the 1970s, but they are now subject to criticism from trade unions and chemical plant owners for their practices.

The danger of market hangovers from compensation deals has also been learned by certain companies in individual transactions. Fiat, for example, participated in the construction of the Togliatti auto plant in the Soviet Union with the assumption that models produced at the plant would be obsolete by the time the Comecon domestic markets absorbed production. Soon after the plant came on-stream, however, Lada models (Fiat analogues) began showing up on hard currency markets at what was considered by some as dumping prices.

Because of the problem of competition, Western companies sometimes consider a joint venture preferable to compensation. In a joint venture, the Western concern owns an equity interest in production facilities, and so has relatively greater control of the manufacture of products and market distribution. Unlike a compensation arrangement, which has a fixed schedule for expiration and guaranteed payment for technology and equipment, a joint venture requires a long-term presence and a risk on investments. In addition, in those countries where direct foreign investments are allowed, joint venture laws are sometimes ambiguous in such crucial areas as taxation and repatriation of profits.

It may be useful here to make a distinction, as far as it can be made, between *cooperation* and *compensation*. Eastern trade organizations typically refer to any compensation agreement as "industrial coopera-tion." The reason for this is largely to place an attractive mantel on the transaction with the implication that both sides of the bargain benefit equally. The Western participant, however, often views the buy-back of resultant products as an unpleasant obligation that must be submitted to in order to make a sale, and so prefers to refer to the transaction as "compensation." This, of course, is not always the case.

In contrast, the Economic Commission of Europe (ECE) is more stringent in its definition of industrial cooperation. All compensation agreements do not qualify, only those that "include a set of comple-mentary or reciprocally matching operations in production, marketing, development, and transfer of technology" or arrangements that have been established by governmental action in bilateral or multilateral agreements.

When a Western company agrees to buy back goods which it will dispose of through a trading house or its own marketing operation, the practice does not qualify as "industrial cooperation" under the ECE specifications. The types of arrangements that may qualify as falling within the scope of industrial cooperation under the ECE definition are: licensing with payment in resultant products; supply of complete plants or production lines with payment in resultant products; coproduction and specialization; subcontracting; joint ventures; and joint tending, joint construction, or similar projects. The first two activities on this list are, by definition, compensation. The remainder of the activities above, however, may or may not be.

EVIDENCE ACCOUNTS

Evidence accounts are commercial agreements between an exporter and one or more foreign trade organizations (FTOs) from the importing country. Under the agreement the exporter sells a pre-set volume of goods and services to one of the FTOs while simultaneously buying local products from the same or other FTO to balance the account. (The buying company has the right to sell the products anywhere else to realize its profits.) To ensure the balance, all transactions during the term of the agreement (commonly one or more years) are monitored by the country's bank of foreign trade, where the company maintains an evidence account, and a foreign bank designated by the Western firm. In this fashion, companies can find profitable business with FTOs of countries that don't have enough hard or transferable currencies on hand to make purchases. Because of this, the FTO can have access to certain goods it could not otherwise afford.

Eastern Bloc nations often find evidence accounts attractive because they fit well into their central economic-planning systems, and allow a great deal of flexibility in buying Western goods with guaranteed, off-setting, hard currency exports. Evidence accounts also hold certain advantages for Western firms. A broader range of goods is offered than in counterpurchase, protracted negotiations are not necessary on each transaction, and there is no need for the approval of one trade organization for purchase from another. Sales can be conducted on purely commercial considerations, and Eastern goods are not inflated with the knowledge that they are being taken as part of a countertrade arrangement.

In order to enter such an arrangement, however, a Western firm must have a significant trade turnover with the importing country and must have reasonable expectations that bilateral trade will rise rather than decrease under the agreement. The Western party must also be certain that it can use products purchased under the account within its own operations or can dispose of them profitably.

BILATERAL CLEARING AGREEMENTS

When two countries wish to trade with one another without expending foreign currency, they may resort to a bilateral clearing agreement. Under this arrangement, the two governments agree to import a set volume of goods from the other over a specified period of time (usually one year).

Accounts are kept in artificial units bearing the denomination of one currency or another: clearing dollar, Swiss franc, rupee, and so on. By this accounting, the bilateral balance of trade can be monitored, and if too great an imbalance occurs, two-way exchange is stopped until accounts are brought back into line. The degree of trade imbalance

SWITCH TRADING

Since credits in a bilateral clearing agreement are not convertible into currency, the agreement often allows the country with a surplus credit to transfer all or part of its clearing account to a third party. This third party, often a switch trading house, uses the credits to purchase goods from the country in deficit and, through a complicated series of deals often involving barter, finally comes up with goods that can be sold for hard currency. The hard currency proceeds are then transferred to the party with the original account surplus, minus a hefty discount for the third party's troubles.

Switch trading was very popular immediately after World War II. Over time, it has declined in importance; today it is estimated that between 60 to 100 million dollars are transacted in switch trading.

allowed is referred to as the "swing." The swing is specified as a percentage of annual trade volume.

If, at the end of a term, one party has taken a greater value of goods than the other, the account must be brought into balance either by cash payment or by "switch trading." In a switch transaction, the party with trade credit left to its account may transfer this credit to a third party at a discount rate and may receive cash payment or other goods.

3

Negotiating Countertrade

When a countertrade demand is introduced into a negotiation, the Western party finds himself negotiating a sale and a linked purchase simultaneously. The purchase commitment he is asked to make, moreover, is often so uncertain that he does not even know exactly what products he will be buying. The negotiation takes on added elements of risk and difficulty that may make the Western executive balk at his prospects, considering it better to return home without a sale than to take on a burden of unwanted goods that his company may not be able to unload at a profit. For reasons such as these, it is estimated that 90 percent of countertrade proposals fall through before a final agreement is reached.

Western companies that successfully conclude profitable countertrade deals are generally those with broad international trade experience, and with the resources and commitment to pursue lengthy and thorough negotiations, anticipating possible problems and safeguarding against them. The first step in a successful negotiation strategy is to be prepared for countertrade demands by knowing your company's position and, as far as is possible, by knowing the bargaining position of the negotiators you face. Negotiators in communist countries and LDCs often do not introduce countertrade demands until late in the game, but it is important for the Western party to avoid being caught off guard. Before entering negotiations that may involve countertrade, the

Western company should have a clear idea of how large a countertrade commitment it is willing to accept as a percentage of its original sale, and it should have an idea of the types of products it is willing to accept in countertrade. A company may decide, for instance, that it will only accept goods that can be used in its own manufacturing operations or that can be marketed through its existing organization. On the other hand, it may decide that goods unrelated to its own operation will be acceptable. If the company decides it is willing to accept goods not within the scope of its own operation, it should determine whether to employ a trading house to dispose of the products (building the trader's commission into the price of the original sale), whether it will market the goods through an existing department of its company, or whether it will set up a new department or subsidiary to handle the purchase and marketing of countertrade goods. (These alternatives of organizing for countertrade will be discussed in greater detail in a later chapter.)

It is also of crucial importance for the Western company to know as much as possible about its trading partner. Research into the organizational structure of trade within a Centrally Planned Economy (CPE) may provide valuable insight into ways of obtaining desired goods for countertrade, and a study of the country's economic five-year plan may shed light on the priority of one's export product, and thus clarify the company's bargaining position. Information concerning the reliability of a country or trade organization and the gambits and ploys it is likely to exercise in negotiating countertrade may be gleaned from discussions with other businessmen who have concluded agreements in the area, or from other trading houses, businesses, and banks.

NEGOTIATING THE COMMITMENT TO COUNTERTRADE

In negotiating a sale with a trade organization in a CPE, the Western negotiator should make every effort to ascertain as early in the talks as possible whether countertrade will enter into the terms of the agreement. In many cases, the foreign trade organization will attempt to negotiate the deal's price on a cash basis. Then, after receiving a final price quote from the Western company, it will spring a demand for countertrade. FTOs in Eastern Europe have been known to inform

Western negotiators at the last minute "with profound regret" that authorities on the ministry level have dictated that they must demand a countertrade commitment in order to make the purchase.

Another gambit that has been employed by East European FTOs is sometimes referred to as "the double trapdoor." The FTO negotiates a purchase under cash terms, receives a final price quote, and then informs the Western company that it must demand countertrade for a percentage of the purchase. After the Western company has acceded to this demand, the FTO informs the Western negotiators that authorities have shifted their position and will allow the purchase to be made in hard currency. The FTO then asks for a reduction of the previously quoted price, since the expenses associated with countertrade are no longer involved.

A Western negotiator must protect himself from these ploys by deferring a final price quote for a sale until an agreement has been reached on the terms and conditions of the sale. If terms are agreed upon early in the negotiations, the Western company may request a written protocol agreement. If the negotiators on the other side decline to be party to such a protocol, it is a good indication that countertrade will enter the negotiations further down the road, and that appropriate preparations should be made.

A company willing to accept countertrade obligations must estimate the cost of disposing of the goods, and include this cost in the final price quoted for its original sale. This may be the cost of a discount to a trading house for assuming the countertrade obligation, or it may be the aggregate cost of marketing the product—transportation, storage, insurance, price discount, and so on.

Trade organizations in CPEs usually insist upon penalties for failure to fulfill countertrade obligations, usually ranging from about 5 to 15 percent. A Western company that does not wish to deal with countertrade goods may consider this penalty as one option. By simply padding the sale's price to absorb the amount of the penalty, the Western party may make its profit from the sale, pay the penalty, and dispense with its obligation.

Exercising this option, however, may jeopardize a company's reputation in a market country, and its prospects for further sales. For example, if the FTO of a CMEA or a company of a developing nation demands countertrade partly as a means to fulfill export quotas, it may suffer serious reprisals from the ministry level if the countertrade exports do not occur. The FTO or company of the developing country would then, understandably, resent the defaulting Western party and avoid further dealings with the firm. It is best, therefore, to ascertain from the appropriate officials whether or not buying out of an obligation is acceptable before opting for penalty payment, if future sales in that market are a concern.

When negotiating the amount of the countertrade commitment, it is important to remember that trade entities in CPEs operate under secret government directives. Negotiators usually begin with a demand for a 50 to 100 percent countertrade commitment, but this is normally only a starting point for bargaining. A skilled negotiator can often reduce the demand by one-half, and it is not unheard of for an initial demand of 100 percent countertrade to be negotiated to 20 or 30 percent. Actual demands for countertrade vary from country to country and from FTO to FTO, but a chief determining factor is the priority of the import in the original sale.

Imports necessary to fulfillment of five-year plans may be purchased without countertrade commitments (unless the cost exceeds allocations of hard currency), while consumer goods not included in the plan often require a 100 percent countertrade commitment. Planned imports of low-priority technical products fall between these extremes, averaging between 40 and 70 percent, and planned imports of consumer goods carry relatively higher demands, averaging between 60 and 80 percent.

SELECTING COUNTERTRADE GOODS

Once a Western company has decided to accept countertrade as a condition on a transaction, it must take on the task of finding goods that can be disposed of profitably. In CMEA countries, this task is becoming increasingly difficult. Only a few years ago, it was still possible to find raw materials such as coal or metal ores to purchase in fulfillment of countertrade obligations. Today, these goods are reserved for hard currency sales except in rare cases in which the imports from the West are of the highest priority. In most developing countries raw materials can be obtained, since countertrade is demanded to obtain a price different from that available on the open market. Since raw materials and commodities can be marketed through established channels at prices that are universally standardized by such indexes as the London or Chicago exchange, they can be disposed of with a minimum effort and pose fewer problems in the areas of quality control, pricing, and after-sale servicing. The cost of disposing of these goods through a trading house is therefore relatively inexpensive, often involving a discount of 5 percent or less.

The Western negotiator today, however, is more likely to find among the countertrade offerings by the FTO of a CMEA, manufactured products or those from developing countries such as consumer goods, and electrical and technical products or machinery. These products are produced by a relatively obsolescent design and often do not enjoy a good reputation in Western markets. Because of their low quality or lack of demand in world markets, they cannot be used to generate hard currency through direct sales and so are earmarked for countertrade. Trading houses charge discounts that average 15 to 30 percent on these goods and 40 percent discounts are not unusual.

LINKAGE

As a general rule, the Western negotiator in a countertrade transaction will want to press for the widest possible range of goods to choose from. Possible ranges of countertrade product offerings include:

1. Only products from the purchasing FTO or company in the original sale.
2. Only products from the industrial ministry that controls the purchasing FTO.
3. Any products offered in the purchasing country.
4. A certain proportion of the obligations fulfilled with purchases from the purchasing FTO, and the remainder fulfilled with purchases from other FTOs under the same ministry.
5. A proportion of the obligation fulfilled with deliveries from the

original buyer FTO, the remainder with any other deliveries of the country's domestic products.

Because of the penchant for bilateralism on the part of Eastern economic planners, an FTO will often press for a countertrade obligation that can only be fulfilled with reciprocal deliveries from the buyer in the original sale. Depending upon the relative priority of the goods offered by the Western company, among other factors, the range of counter-trade offerings from which to choose can be expanded to include products from other FTOs as well. This sort of arrangement is referred to as "countertrade linkage." Generally, the Western party will consider an obligation to purchase from among any products of the purchasing country to be the ideal condition, but the purchasing FTO will usually insist that at least some portion of the counterpurchase be chosen from among its own product lines.

The Western negotiator may also press for a clause ensuring that all purchases from trading entities designated in the obligation will qualify as countertrade. It has often occurred that a Western purchasing agent, after prolonged search, finds goods that his company can market to an identified customer only to be informed that the intended purchase could not be credited against the company's countertrade obligations because of the absence of a specific linkage clause in the contract.

Similarly, the Western party may want to negotiate for purchases exceeding its countertrade obligation to be credited against future company sales. Some Eastern European trading entities have been known to allow purchasing credits to be transferred to third parties as well, but these are isolated cases and rarely allow for the transfer of the full value of sales. On a $100,000 sale, for instance, an FTO may allow a $50,000 countertrade credit to be transferred to a third party.

LISTS

When negotiating the selection of countertrade goods in a CMEA country, a Western company is commonly supplied with a published countertrade list by an FTO. These lists are sometimes outdated, with many or most of the items no longer available. Upon request, the FTO may provide a shorter, more accurate list of products offered as countertrade. Even these items, however, are often not available when the Western firm tries to order them. Bids for hard currency sales will always supplant countertrade deliveries and goods offered as counter-trade change according to market demand. A Western company that has regularly been buying certain textile articles in fulfillment of counter-trade obligations, for instance, may suddenly find these unavailable if the products become competitive in hard currency markets. One of the best policies is for the Western purchasing agents to cultivate close relations, not only with the special FTO department that handles countertrade, but with sales departments as well, with an eye to locating desired products throughout the year. Beyond these FTO contacts, Western executives have often found there to be no substitute for deep involvement with manufacturers in the Eastern country.

This type of involvement usually requires a long-term arrangement with the supplying FTO. By committing itself to such a long-term agreement, the Western company can increase its leverage in choosing products. In addition, long-term buying can facilitate arrangements for manufacturers to produce "made to order" goods as countertrade, or to expand the production of goods that they would otherwise not offer as countertrade in order to fill guaranteed orders. Long-term arrange-ments also serve to enhance the reputation of the Western company and increase its opportunities for future sales.

CHOICE OF PRODUCTS

A company's choice of countertrade products, of course, will depend upon customers it has identified, the nature and scope of its operations, its marketing capacities, and other factors. Generally speaking, how-ever, the preferability of product types can be rated as follows:

1. *Raw materials*—These can be marketed through established channels at standardized prices and pose relatively low risk.
2. *Products that can be used in the company's own operations*— Component parts or simple tools that can be absorbed by the Western company into its operations do not involve the cost of

marketing the goods or the payment of a discount to a trading house.

3. *Goods related to the company's own product lines*—Since these products can be disposed of through the existing marketing organization of the Western company or its suppliers, they do not require expenditures for trading house discounts or other costs associated with finding a third-party buyer and transferring the goods.

4. *Manufactured products unrelated to a company's operation*— These products are generally the least preferred because they must be either assigned to a trading house for disposal at a discount, or marketed to a third party with associated costs.

Among manufactured goods offered as countertrade, products that require no after-sales service or parts are generally preferred. Such products as ball bearings or simple electric hand tools are more easily sold on Western markets than are complicated machinery or engineering goods, where the market is already saturated.

4

Contract Considerations

Except in the case of pure barter, countertrade transactions have traditionally taken the form of a "contractual triangle." This is composed of three separate legal instruments that, when taken together, establish the terms and conditions of the deal. The three points of this triangle are: (1) the original contract for a Western sale, (2) the countertrade contract which sets the original seller's obligation to purchase goods from the buyer in the first contract, and (3) the protocol that serves to link the two contracts.

The protocol, or as it is referred to in Britain, the "head of agreement," is drafted first. This is an "agreement to agree" under which each party commits itself to enter into its respective contract to purchase the other party's goods with hard currency. (This commitment may be secured with the use of standby letters of credit or a performance bond.) In addition to its primary function of assuring each party that one contract will not be signed without the other, the protocol may also serve the critical function of assuring the seller in the first contract that his obligations under the second contract will terminate in the event of nonperformance or cancellation of the original purchase. The use of a protocol, however, is by no means universal. Increasingly, as countertrade becomes more common, clauses in the two contracts themselves are used to link the legal instruments together.

The first contract in the countertrade arrangement is a standard sale agreement not unlike a cash-for-goods agreement. In the case of compensation, this contract is far from simple or standard, but its complexity arises from the technology transfer factor and is not unique to countertrade.

The second or "countertrade" contract sometimes calls for payment in hard currency for deliveries. It differs, however, in setting terms for a purchase obligation. It is most commonly an agreement for the purchase of goods at a later date, or over a period of time, rather than a simple agreement for the purchase of specified goods according to a definite schedule of delivery and payment.

It is of crucial importance that the countertrade contract be drafted clearly and unambiguously in all of its provisions, and that nothing be left to common sense or to later interpretation. In transactions with nonmarket countries, the Western firm will often be presented with a standard "frame contract," which the foreign negotiators will want to hold to rather closely. The Western negotiator, however, will often find it to his advantage to press for alterations in the provisions or for additional provisions to be included in the agreement.

In developing countries a Western company is often advised to draft its own contract rather than accept the standard document issued by the purchasing agency or ministry. This has two advantages: familiarity with the subtler points of the contract, and inversely, the avoidance of unexpected or undetected pitfalls. The terms, however, should be familiar to both parties.

The non-Western trading partner will probably feel more comfortable if the provisions of the contract offered by the Western firm are based on clauses taken from agreements already in effect between trading entities of the two participating countries. Copies of previously signed contracts involving the purchase of goods usually can be obtained from other businessmen or officials of the Department of Commerce or the Department of State, through their respective country desk officers.

There are seven key features of a countertrade contract. Each should be given special consideration during the drafting process.

1. *Separation of contracts.* One of the most crucial reasons for the use of two separate contracts is the need for independent legal instruments in order to obtain financing and credit-risk guarantees from banks or other institutions. Another reason is that the use of two contracts allows for different maturities for the original purchase and for the obligation for reciprocal purchase. A third reason for dual contracts is the need to keep payments for the original sale unencumbered by the conditions of the obligation to accept counterdeliveries.

A Western company entering into a countertrade transaction under a single contract could place itself in the dangerous position of having to fulfill its countertrade obligation in order to receive payment for its export sale. In a worst-case scenario, the foreign trade entity could deliberately make no products available for export to fulfill the countertrade obligation, and thus claim the right to withhold payment for goods received from the Western company under the contract. Of course, such behavior could no doubt have an effect on future commercial relations between the two parties.

Even with the use of two contracts, the Western party must be careful to protect its right to payment for its export, independent of its obligation to counterpurchase. To this end, it is advisable that the Western sale contract contain no reference to the countertrade contract. Also, any references to the Western export in the second countertrade contract should be drafted so that the two agreements do not merge into a single legal instrument.

A common method of ensuring the independence of the Western export is to include a special clause in the countertrade contract to that effect. This clause will usually appear as a provision that, in case of the Western party's nonfulfillment of its countertrade obligation, the payment of a penalty will release the Western party from any further obligation or responsibility.

In one sense, however, the Western party will want a degree of linkage between the agreement for the Western export and the agreement to counterpurchase. In the event that the Western sale is cancelled or delayed, the Western party will usually want the option of being released from its obligation to purchase the other party's goods.

This right of release is sometimes accomplished through the protocol, which may call for the cancellation of one contract if the other contract is cancelled or delayed. A connection between the Western sale and the countertrade obligation may also be made by a reference to the Western sale in the clause defining the Western party's obligation to purchase. This can be done either by explicit wording that states the obligation to be pursuant to the sale in the first contract, or it can be accomplished by stating the amount of the obligation as a percentage of the value of the Western sale.

If the latter procedure is followed, the obligation should be stated as a percentage of the Western sales price FOB, so that the obligation will not be inflated as a proportion of the total import cost to the other party including shipping, insurance, duties, and so on.

2. The obligation to purchase. The countertrade contract will commonly contain a provision defining the value of the reciprocal purchase to be made by the seller in the first contract, the time period during which the purchase must be made and, in transactions with nonmarket countries, the trade organizations from which the goods must be purchased.

If, as in some cases (particularly in compensation deals), the products to be purchased as countertrade are to be specified in the contract, they should be described exhaustively and in minute detail with complete and unequivocal definitions of quality standards.

More often, however, the purchase obligation provision of a countertrade contract will call for goods to be selected from a certain range of products for later purchase. In these cases, it is generally advantageous for the Western party to have a broad as possible range of products from which to choose.

It is even possible to secure a linkage clause providing for purchases from any organization in the target country to apply to its countertrade obligation. In CMEA countries, however, the Eastern party will probably insist that at least a portion of the countertrade obligation be satisfied with purchases from its buyer.

An alternative to linkage would be to select a list of goods offered by the nontrading partner, and to specify them in the purchase obligation of the countertrade contract. If they are specified, however, a clause must be included in the contract, releasing the Western party from its countertrade obligation if products ordered are not delivered according to schedule and according to quality specifications.

In CMEA countries, negotiators are rarely willing to grant these guarantees of delivery. For this reason, experienced East-West traders counsel against narrowing countertrade options by specifying a product list. In the absence of firm guarantees, a specific purchase obligation may put the Western party in a position either to accept the chosen goods (regardless of delivery delays or inferior quality) or to pay a penalty for nonfulfillment of its obligation.

The Western party should press for as lengthy a period as possible to purchase countertrade goods. A longer obligation period allows the buyer time to locate customers for countertrade goods and reduces storage costs. Although the Eastern negotiator may ask for a time limit of 6 to 12 months for counterpurchase obligations, this can usually be extended through patient and skillful negotiation to a period of 2 to 3 years. In any case, the time limit for a counterpurchase should extend beyond the period of financing for the original Western sale.

3. Penalties. The Eastern party to a transaction will usually insist on a provision that will impose a penalty on the Western party for nonfulfillment of its purchase obligation. This penalty is stated as a percentage of the unfulfilled portion of the obligation and typically ranges from 10 to 15 percent in Eastern Europe or the Soviet Union. The East Bloc negotiator will, in addition, insist on a guarantee for the total amount of possible penalties to be issued by a Western bank to the state bank of the Eastern partner. Under this guarantee, the Western bank transfers the amount of the penalty to the state bank, unconditionally and without recourse, at the end of the Western company's countertrade obligation for the unfilled portion of the obligation.

The Western party should have a clause included in the contract, stipulating that payment of a penalty releases him from any further obligation to purchase, and from any other claims of the Eastern party. FTOs in certain CMEA countries have been known to demand specific performance, even after a penalty has been paid.

4. Pricing. Since countertrade contracts usually involve either the purchase of unspecified goods, or the purchase of specified goods over a long term, pricing provisions normally contain pricing formulas rather than set prices.

In compensation agreements, the pricing formula often involves periodic review or renegotiation of the product value, typically at intervals of three to nine months. If the buy-back product in such an arrangement is agricultural goods or raw materials, the price may be set as the value of the goods according to a mutually recognized index at the time of the order. An alternative in transactions of this sort is to set the price for deliveries in the contract draft with a formula that calls for a review of the price if the value of the goods rises above, or falls below, a certain value on the mutually recognized index for the goods.

If the buy-back products are finished or semifinished goods, the pricing formula may call for price readjustment periodically, and/or when market conditions change. Some conditions that may call for price review under such an arrangement might be a change in raw material prices, a change in demand for the product on world markets, or a change in political conditions.

In transactions that involve a commitment to purchase unspecified products (most counterpurchase agreements), a clearly defined pricing formula should be employed to prevent prices (often grossly inflated) from being set by the foreign trading entity.

A common formula is to define the price of the goods as "the acceptable international price at the time of purchase." The application for this kind of formula is a comparison of the price paid to the supplier by other customers in Western markets for the same product.

Another common formula may read "fair market value of goods in first party's country" (or a percentage above or below this value). This formula could be applied by a price comparison with similar goods of equal quality available to the Western party, under competitive terms of delivery and payment, from other foreign suppliers.

The method of applying a pricing formula, as well as the formula itself, should be clearly defined and as specific as possible. A provision should also be included that specifies that both parties shall submit to arbitration in the event that there is a disagreement over the application of the formula.

5. Quality. Manufactured and semimanufactured products taken in countertrade often have been of inferior quality. It is therefore necessary for the Western party to be especially careful in drafting provisions for quality standards, penalties, and right to inspect.

All specifications regarding goods exchanged should be attached to the contract as an addendum and referred to in the provision.

For many types of products (high-technology components, machinery, or equipment parts, etc.) items that do not conform completely to specifications are totally or nearly worthless. For these products, the quality guarantee clause should unequivocally state that nonconforming deliveries will not be accepted. An alternative sometimes employed is a provision stating that nonconforming products will be returned to the supplier for retooling or repair (at the supplier's expense), or that the purchaser will remake the product to specification, and charge such repair to the supplier.

In other cases, it may be appropriate to assign penalties for degrees of nonfulfillment. These penalties, of course, must be defined very carefully in reference to the most detailed index of specifications.

In countertrade contracts that do not specify products to be purchased, the standard for deliveries is often expressed in such terms as "export quality." The application should be defined as clearly as possible. The countertrade contract should provide the Western party the right to inspect purchased goods before delivery. In some cases (usually in compensation arrangements), Western company personnel may inspect goods at the manufacturing site. If this is not allowed, a provision should allow the purchaser to inspect goods before shipment. A provision that would allow the Western party to choose a neutral surveyor to assess product quality may have to be included.

6. Distribution. Sometimes a Western firm finds a customer for products it can purchase as countertrade, then discovers that the other party in the countertrade deal has already granted an exclusive distributorship to a third party for the area of the planned resale. The Western firm must then either abandon the transaction or pay a commission on the resale to the area distributor.

To avoid this problem, the Western party should include a provision in the countertrade contract that either allows the buyer to market countertrade goods in Western markets without interference from the foreign trade entity, or allows for exclusive distribution in certain markets.

7. Transferability of countertrade obligation. The countertrade contract should contain, either in the recitals or the provision stating the Western party's purchase obligation, a clause allowing the purchaser to assign his countertrade obligation to a third party. This clause will sometimes indicate the party or parties to whom the obligation may be assigned (e.g., a trading house). In other cases, the third party will not be designated.

Even if the Western firm plans to use the countertrade goods in its own operations, or market the goods without the aid of a trading house, this provision should still be drafted into the countertrade agreement. Transferability is an important option to reserve in case of unforeseen contingencies.

5

Organizing for Countertrade

The ability of a Western company to efficiently dispose of goods received in countertrade will often determine the profitability of the deal. If the Western company has been successful in negotiating the contract, it will have already included in the price of the goods it will provide the cost of disposing of the items received in countertrade. Often the least complicated form of countertrade in terms of disposal occurs when the Western firm can use the item received as an input for its production or is capable of marketing the item through its own trade network. This, however, is not usually the case. As a result, the firm is required to find a market for the acquired goods and/or materials.

THE DECISION TO USE A TRADING HOUSE

For a firm that rarely deals in countertrade and has little desire to establish its own countertrade unit, it is usually preferable to contract the services of a trading house. The first step is to select a trading house whose specializations in terms of product and area of geographical expertise suit one's needs.

The Department of Commerce's International Trade Administration describes four primary functions of trading houses:[3]

- Marketing, including representation;
- Transportation, including warehousing and insurance;
- Finance, including investment management and credit extension;
- Manufacture, including upgrading of commodities.

Some trading houses work as brokers trying to bring together sellers and buyers of particular items. Their primary activity is to keep abreast of the needs of companies in a particular industry and to be able to come up with supplies of inputs for production.

Others play a more active role. They will act as principals, buying and reselling the items. If the trading company does not have a customer at the time of the acquisition, it will stockpile the goods for a future sale.

It is possible to work with a trading company on a consulting basis. The Western exporter might hire the trading house as an adviser to provide information as to what type of items should be obtained to fulfill a countertrade obligation. The trading houses that specialize in one particular country or small group of countries will usually possess a large reservoir of expertise to steer Western firms away from undesirable goods that will be difficult to resell.

The profit margins of trading companies are generally said to be 1 to 4 percent in low-risk items and 15 to 20 percent in higher risk categories. Some Western companies, however, claim the rates are actually much higher. In addition to the disadvantage of having either to pay a commission or to sell the countertraded items at a discount, there is the negative feature that the Western firm will fail to gain knowledge of the market when it sells, and therefore will continue to be dependent on the services of a trading house. If the use of trading houses proves unsatisfactory, the Western firm has the option of establishing its own countertrade unit, which many companies have proceeded to do.

THE IN-HOUSE TRADING ORGANIZATION

In-house trading units are becoming more and more common in large U.S. multinationals. This is because in the past such firms have either been forced to use the services of trading houses or abstain from deals involving countertrade. The first policy resulted in a loss of profit, the second meant a loss in potential sales.

Generally, literature on countertrade identifies three or four types of countertrade units. The International Trade Commission, for example, classifies them into profit center trading companies, direct countertrade organizations, indirect countertrade organizations, and countertrade purchasing organizations.[4] Such a breakdown is useful, but since the nature of a company's business is likely to evolve over a period of time, it is difficult to consistently fit a firm squarely into one category.

A company that deals extensively in countertrade often establishes its own countertrade trading company. In addition to helping its parent company fulfill the countertrade obligations, the countertrade unit takes on additional clients. The rationale for this is obvious: since the trading company has acquired an expertise in countertrade, it might as well market its skills and knowledge. Such a company remains affiliated with the parent firm but is usually autonomous. It may abstain from working with companies that deal in commodities similar to those of its parent. It usually is capable of providing services in all aspects of international trade and usually maintains its own market research division.

Philbro is an example of a profit-center trading company. It is the world's largest and most diversified trading company specializing in raw materials. Worldwide, it maintains 50 offices. While the firm began initially to find and market products for its parents, it eventually expanded to dominate its field.[5]

The second type of countertrade organ, the direct countertrade organization, functions similarly to the profit-center, trading company, except that it works only for the parent company. It is not a self-sustaining corporate entity. Its only concern is to market the items received in countertrade by the parent company.

The indirect countertrade organization acts primarily as a middleman between its parent company and firms that are end-users of the goods received in countertrade. It is found most often in companies that receive uniform countertrade products from LDCs such as oil, metals, and food products. It does not usually perform the function of studying and advising what products to obtain in countertrade or play a role in marketing the items.

The last form of countertrade unit, the countertrade purchasing organization, differs from the other types in that it seeks only goods and services that can be used for the operation of its parent company. It is most often found in firms that operate factories individually or on a joint basis in foreign countries. The ITC pointed out in its report on countertrade that this type of unit sometimes has difficulty coordinating with the other purchasing units of its company that are obtaining goods by more traditional means. Especially in East Bloc countries, problems arise in obtaining goods on time to be used in the production process. This can cause bootlenecks.

Many different factors determine how a company should organize its countertrade activity: size of countertrade activity, type of product produced, duration of contract, and company size are just a few. It is necessary to have the structure of the countertrade unit fit the particular needs of the firm.

FINANCE

In countertrade transactions both with East Bloc and developing countries, the Western firm usually is forced to extend credit to its customer to allow for the purchase of its products. This is because the importer is either unable or unwilling to use its own resources.

MID- TO LONG-TERM FINANCING

Firms engaged in countertrade must be certain to include the finance cost in the price of goods or services it is providing. For compensation arrangements, Western banks involved often utilize a criterion of "project financing" rather than concern themselves with the economic position of the parties involved. The banks examine the profitability of the deal. For example, they may demand to know how and where the items received in countertrade will be marketed.

In large commercial transactions, government credits often play a substantial role. In order to avoid a credit war in trade subsidies, the OECD nations have a set of guidelines governing the rates at which loans can be extended. The world's nations are divided into "poor" (per capita income of less than $1,000), "intermediate" ($1,000 to $3,000), and "rich" (over $3,000) nations. The poorer the nation, the larger the subsidy permitted. In practice this system does not work as planned because of varying government policies encouraging exports. The specific guidelines are:

- A minimum down payment of 15 percent regardless of the destination of the export;
- A maximum repayment period of 5 to 10 years (depending on the income level of the recipient of the initial export);
- For credits over 5 years, minimum interest rates of 8.75 percent for rich countries, 8.5 percent for intermediate, and 7.75 for poor ones;
- For credits of 2 to 5 years, the interest rates are 8.5 percent for rich countries, 8 percent for intermediate, and 7.5 percent for poor;
- Local costs are covered up to the value of exported goods and services.[6]

In addition to funds subsidized through government and commercial banks, funds for projects may be obtained from institutions such as the World Bank, the Islamic Bank, and various regional organizations.

6

The Current Countertrade Environment

INTRODUCTION

In the first five chapters of this monograph, a generic description of countertrade has been presented. Countertrade, however, is not a process codified by specific laws. It is a mechanism utilized to accomplish trade under conditions of insufficient hard currency. For countertrade to function, a partial coincidence of wants has to exist. One party will want to import a good, service, or technology and the other party must be willing to accept in return as partial or full payment something other than convertible currency.

One must always bear in mind the importance of uncertainty in the environment in which countertrade occurs. The key determinants of countertrade are the parties' needs to complete a transaction and their relative negotiating skills. There are many other variables: changing import requirements, the need of both parties to clear inventories, the availability of hard currency, and the relationship of the importer to its government bureaucracy, to name a few.

THE EAST BLOC'S COUNTERTRADE ENVIRONMENT

In the 1970s, the Soviet Union and the nations of Eastern Europe embarked on industrial modernization programs. With their nonconvertible currencies, trade on a cash-for-goods basis was limited. Moreover, the system of maintaining "material balances" encouraged economic units to think in terms of physical amounts of products, as opposed to "monetary value." The shortage of hard currency led the central economic planning organs to demand countertrade obligations on foreign imports from the West. In a sense, these countries desired to make trade with the West resemble trade within the East Bloc, where it is basically countertrade between countries using "transferable rubles" for accounting purposes.

The Soviet and Eastern European demands for capital goods from the West surged; in theory, the expanded industrial capacity acquired would be able to generate revenues which could finance these imports, but poor implementation of the programs and lack of demand for the East Bloc products resulted in a serious imbalance-of-trade problem.

Possessing limited hard currency reserves, the Soviets and the Eastern Europeans turned increasingly to foreign credits to finance their deficits. The result was a six-and-one-half times increase in the debt of the CMEA nations from $12 billion in 1973 to $78 billion ($20 billion for the Soviet Union and $58 billion for the Eastern Europeans) in 1982.[7]

Although the imports of equipment (roughly 35 percent of CMEA's imports) and raw materials failed to bring about the planned increase of exports, the East Bloc has been unwilling to abandon or to seriously alter its strategy, which has proceeded too far to turn back. Under these conditions, the central planning apparatus in each country has demanded that its foreign trade organizations impose countertrade obligations.

As mentioned above, each countertrade deal is a unique transaction. While it is useful to observe the trend in the growing scale of the demands made by each CMEA country, it is the particular nature of each deal contemplated that will determine the size of the countertrade obligation. In the paragraphs to follow, a general description of the compensation rates currently asked for and negotiated by the CMEA states is presented.

BULGARIA

According to a 1981 report of the OECD, Bulgaria has increased its demands for countertrade. In the past, Bulgarian FTOs might initially have postured for 100 percent countertrade. They would negotiate a final agreement at 40 to 50 percent. The Bulgarians have changed their tactics somewhat. They do not always open with a demand for 100 percent countertrade, but they are less willing to reduce the final countertrade level below the 50 to 70 percent range. Differences, of course, exist from sector to sector and trade organization to trade organization. Industrial goods handled by Machinoexport and Techno-import usually involve a 20 to 40 percent countertrade obligation. Neftochim and Industrial import, which handle more general goods, have obtained countertrade obligations in the 10 to 30 percent range. In contrast, importation of nonessential consumer goods is not considered vital enough to warrant the use of scarce hard currency, and counter-trade obligations in this area reach the 80 to 100 percent figure.[8]

The goods offered by Bulgarian foreign trade organizations can be of low quality and could not be sold to the West under normal trade conditions. Electrical and transport equipment, as well as chemicals (plastics, synthetic fibers, fertilizer, and base chemicals) are usually offered in return for Western imports.[9]

CZECHOSLOVAKIA

While the pressure exerted by Czech foreign trade enterprises has been increasing recently, the incidence of Czech countertrade remains toward the lower end of the spectrum of East Bloc countries. The Czechs would prefer that a Western firm receive goods from the foreign trade organization that has made the import, but allow linkage so that the Western party can purchase something from another enterprise. Two organizations, TRANSACTA and FINCOM, help Western companies find Czech products that will be acceptable for trade. The Czechs prefer compensation to buy-back arrangements, especially if it encourages increased cooperation between Czech and Western enterprises.[10]

The countertrade rates for Czech organizations vary from enterprise to enterprise, which probably indicates the relative "exportability" of their products. Two organizations importing heavy machinery, Kovo and Strojimport, have countertrade rates of 10 to 25 percent and 10 to 20 percent, respectively. Strojimport and Pragoinvest, which deal with lighter equipment, have higher rates of 20 to 30 percent and 50 percent, respectively.[11]

EAST GERMANY

As one might suspect, the GDR, the most industrially advanced state in CMEA, has less need for countertrade since its products are more likely to have hard currency markets. The goods offered for countertrade by the GDR are among the highest quality in the Eastern Bloc. As in the case of Czechoslovakia, German authorities prefer buy-back or compensation as the form of countertrade, since it is likely to result from the purchase of equipment or licenses.[12]

GDR countertrade agreements utilizing counterpurchasing have averaged 50 percent of the total value of the import from the West. These arrangements typically involve metals from the East German FTOs, Unitechna, Technocommerz, and W.M.W. Export-Import. Imports, which the current plan does not provide for, usually involve countertrade provisions of 80 to 100 percent. The highest countertrade rates, at 100 percent plus financing, are for compensation agreements. These agreements typically provide for the building and equipping of complete industrial plants.[13]

HUNGARY

For a long time Hungary avoided using countertrade. Recently, however, the pressure has been mounting. Still, the rates demanded and obtained in countertrade negotiations remain relatively low by East European standards. Nikex, Technoimpex, and Transelectro, which deal in industrial goods, typically operate with 15 to 30 percent countertrade rates. Sixty percent countertrade demands are not unusual for low-priority items; 100 percent rates are common for unscheduled imports of consumer items.[14]

Officially, a Western firm is free to choose products from any FTO to fulfill its counterpurchase obligation, but there is a tendency by the FTO to try to limit its foreign trading partner to products of the enterprise that is receiving the import. The goods made available by Hungarian enterprises, unlike those of other Eastern European countries, are not shoddy products which cannot otherwise be sold, but are available as a result of overproduction.

POLAND

Countertrade with Poland faces an uncertain future. The government of Jaruzelski cannot continue the import policies that began under Gierek. Poland was unique in Eastern Europe in that it imported not only capital goods from the West, but also large amounts of food and consumer items. Western banks and governments probably will not continue to extend Poland the additional loans it needs to perpetuate the industrial modernization program. Because of the upheaval caused by labor unrest and compounded by widespread economic mismanagement, Poland has become an unattractive trading partner for the West. Desirable goods for countertrade are simply not available. Poland's uncertain future discourages Western firms from initiating new compensation agreements, since there is no guarantee that they will obtain what is promised.

Before the recent upheaval, Poland tried to cover the expense of its major import projects with compensation agreements, often worth 100 percent or more of the import price. Other industrial goods carried countertrade rates of a smaller magnitude. For example, Polimex-Cekor, Varimex, Elektrim, and Ramafet usually signed contracts where there was a 20 to 30 percent countertrade provision. Other imports such as machine tools and intermediate goods usually carried a 30 to 50 percent countertrade obligation.[15] Poland had been the East European country possessing the closest industrial relations with the West. Its future cannot be predicted at this time.

ROMANIA

Romania is the only East European country with specific countertrade guidelines established by its industrial ministries. Since 1981, Romanian FTCs have demanded 100 percent countertrade as a result of current regulations. Romanian foreign trade organizations receive counter-trade goals in conjunction with their export targets from the central planning authorities.[16]

Romania pays for essential imports in hard currency, but lower priority purchases require countertrade, sometimes at a 100 percent rate. The level of countertrade demanded varies from sector to sector and from case to case. For example, firms in the engineering area such as Machinoexport and Electronum usually receive a 50 percent counter-trade provision in their agreements; 35 to 50 percent is typical for the purchase of machinery in the chemical industry, and 30 to 50 percent for light industry.[17]

Romanian goods are difficult to market. Furniture, clothing, ma-chinery, and electrical goods are most easy for Western firms to dispose of. Usually the terms for counterpurchases are negotiable, but accord-ing to the Department of Commerce, Romania is thinking of specifying the volume and value of the product, which would have to be taken within a year of the signing of the contract. Nonetheless, while Romania may formally be stricter than other CMEA countries in outlining require-ments, a considerable amount of leeway exists for Western companies to negotiate the specifics of their agreements. How favorable the terms the Western firm can obtain will ultimately depend on how essential its product is and the availability of competitors who may be willing to provide similar goods under different terms.

THE SOVIET UNION

The Soviet Union is the East Bloc's largest countertrader. Its foreign trade organizations want countertrade whenever a contract's value is greater than $1 million, even though it can pay in cash. The counter-purchase rates normally obtained vary between 20 and 30 percent and for compensation agreements, 30 to 60 percent. These figures represent an increase over the 1976 levels by a factor of 3 to 4. The Soviets favor compensation agreements where the Western firm receives in exchange for its equipment products such as chemicals or machinery. Soviet countertrade demands are highest for chemicals, light industry, and consumer goods, and lowest for iron, steel, electronics, and machinery.[18]

While the Soviet Union would like to increase Western involvement in the expansion of its manufacture of finished and intermediate products, Western firms and governments are most interested in working with the Soviet Union on developing Soviet energy resources. Under a shroud of controversy, West German banks have extended $6 billion in credit to the Soviet Union to purchase equipment for a new gas pipeline, which will deliver $8 billion annually to customers in Western Europe.

While the Soviet Union has a $20 billion debt to the West, this figure, when examined in light of the size of the Soviet economy ($1.8 trillion) does not appear excessive. The Soviets maintain $30 billion in gold and hard currency reserves so that any project essential to the economy can be financed.[19]

GOODS OFFERED BY CMEA NATIONS

Exhibit 1 displays the classification of countertrade goods offered by the nations of CMEA in countertrade negotiations. Generally machinery, vehicles, chemicals, and raw materials are the most common items given in countertrade. While the quality of goods varies from item to item, the hierarchy of quality tends to be, from best to worst, East German, Czechoslovakian, Hungarian, Soviet, Polish, Romanian, and Bulgarian.

YUGOSLAVIA

Yugoslavia, while geographically located in Eastern Europe, is not politically and economically part of the Soviet Bloc. Its economy is organized along the principle of workers' self-management. Economic

Exhibit 1. Classification of countertrade goods offered, 1980 (given as percent of total).

	Machinery & Vehicles	Chemical & Raw Material Products	Consumer Products	Electrical & Electronic Equipment
Bulgaria	35	20	15	30
Czechoslovakia	50	20	20	10
GDR	35	25	15	25
Hungary	45	15	25	15
Poland	45	25	10	20
Romania	55	15	15	15
Soviet Union	30	40	10	20

SOURCE: Seminar materials of Business International Institute.

planning is also decentralized to a far greater extent than elsewhere in the region.

At the end of 1981, Yugoslavia's foreign debt was $18.4 billion. The central government is determined not to allow this amount to increase. While there are officially no countertrade obligations imposed by Yugoslav regulation, the government encourages compensation agreements and joint enterprises. Western firms by necessity may find countertrade the only means of completing a transaction because of the hard currency constraint. The Yugoslav federal government maintains a large list of export goods that are available for countertrade.

Through the services of Yugoslav banks, it is possible to arrange to fulfill countertrade obligations from a commercial enterprise other than the one receiving the Western firm's export. While it is somewhat easier to deal with Yugoslav companies within the same republic, to minimize the number of Yugoslav parties involved in the deal, it is possible to export to one enterprise in Croatia, for example, and receive goods from Serbia.[20]

CHINA

While China will be discussed here along with the other "East Bloc" countries, its experience with countertrade bears a closer resemblance to that of the developing countries.

China has recently adopted an economic development plan to entice Western businesses with many export opportunities. The Chinese economy, however, as it emerges from years of relative isolation, is ill-prepared to pay for its ambitious modernization program. A major challenge facing Chinese economic planners today is to find the means to acquire foreign technology without an unbearable burden of foreign debt.

When China's pragmatic leadership set out on its course toward modernization in 1978, it envisioned the accomplishment of the "four modernizations"—those of agriculture, industry, national defense, and science—by the year 2000. The first phase of this celebrated modernization drive, the 1976–1981 five-year plan, included some 120 major projects—most of them involving imports, and/or foreign participation.

By 1979, however, it became clear that China's meager hard-currency reserves and her limited capacity to generate hard currency through exports (due to an underdeveloped industrial infrastructure) made it impossible to implement the 1976 five-year plan without a reliance on foreign credits.

The Chinese leadership, for ideological reasons, was averse to such a policy and therefore decided to scale down, postpone, or cancel a large number of major projects under the plan. At the same time, the Chinese leadership embarked upon a three-year "readjustment period," which has been extended into an "indefinite period of readjustment." Under this retrenchment, priority was given to projects that require less foreign exchange, provide a quicker return on investment, and offer greater export earning potential. Thus China decided to live with a slower rate of industrialization and to tie foreign imports closely to the level of exports.

While China continues its large number of bilateral trade contacts with developing countries, it has increasingly looked to the West and Japan to obtain technology for its economy. China has restructured its foreign trade apparatus by creating the Ministry of Foreign Trade and Economic Relations (MOFTER). In the 1980s, the Chinese leadership has three goals that are dependent on closer ties with the industrialized world: (1) the development of the country's offshore oil resources, which could provide hard currency for the import of additional goods, services, and technology; (2) assistance in the production of intermediate products such as iron, steel, and chemicals; and (3) improvement of its light industry, which not only provides exportable items but also makes available consumer goods that are essential to provide workers with incentives for higher productivity.

The Chinese are eager to have their products marketed abroad, and, in contrast to the East Europeans, allow a more active role for their trading partners in assisting with quality control. The Chinese view this assistance as essential for the improvement of their industry.

Because of the low labor costs, many firms have entered into processing agreements with Peking. In the last three years, 6,000 agreements have been signed with foreign concerns for a contract value between 700 and 800 million dollars. Usually these arrangements call for the foreign party to provide equipment, technical assistance, and even some of the raw materials, and the Chinese factory to sell back the output at a discount.[21]

The worldwide recession has discouraged many Western firms from entering into processing/compensation agreements. While China represents a huge market that foreign companies want to penetrate, there is a risk involved for Western firms in encouraging the modernization of China since it might emerge as a commercial competitor. If China emerges as a large supplier of raw materials, crude oil, or labor intensive goods, it may flood the market. China usually requires that only 30 percent of compensation trade output be used domestically; the rest of the foreign trading partner has to dispose of itself.

Chinese countertrade agreements are small in scale compared to those of other East Bloc countries, and its involvement in international trade still exhibits a quality of experimentation. Western companies have experienced problems because of a lack of central control over foreign trade. As a result, companies and regional units are sometimes unable to fulfill the conditions of the contract that they have signed.

THE COUNTERTRADE ENVIRONMENT IN
THE THIRD WORLD

At the end of 1979, the cumulative foreign debt of the developing world (specifically non-oil exporters) stood at $316 billion.[22] Much of this debt is due either directly or indirectly to the eightfold increase in the price of crude oil since 1973. Whereas the industrial world has in large part been able to adjust to its increased oil bill by exporting more to the oil-producing countries, or passing on the price hike to consumers through inflated prices, the states of the developing world have had less success at financing the import of oil.

Over all, from 1970 to 1979, exports and GNP among developing countries increased at a rate sufficient for these states to improve their credit ratings and, consequently, to obtain loans from commercial markets. Still, performances were uneven, and in 1979/1980, the price received for many raw materials began to fall. Furthermore, the recession in the industrial West began to lower the availability of funds for lending institutions to the Third World. The growth in funds lessened; at the same time, the real level of foreign aid to the "hardship" countries decreased.

The net effects of the oil price increases on the Third World are structural readjustments of resources for export promotion and import substitution, a greater dependence on external financing, and slower rates of industrial growth. While such adjustments may strengthen the economic position of each individual state, they further contribute to an overall stagnation of the global economy.

Exhibit 2 displays the balance of payments and debt-servicing situations of a selected number of developing countries. These countries run the gamut in their ability to adjust to the oil shocks. Singapore and Turkey have reacted particularly well. Indonesia, Brazil, and, surprisingly, Mexico have adjusted the least successfully.

It is under this type of balance-of-trade situation that countertrade emerges as one means of dealing with hard-currency shortages and with a country's limited prospects for generating increased demand for its exports. This situation is aggravated by the tendency of LDCs to overvalue their currency above market clearing rates and has led to a shortfall in convertible currencies. A recent ITC study argues that:

> Many LDCs have in the past relied upon elaborate tax rates of exchange and subsidy systems set up to produce the desired mixture of imports and exports. Therefore some degree of currency inconvertibility is necessary to prevent the undoing of the efforts of government planners. The central

Exhibit 2. Balance of payments and debt servicing (selected countries).

	Current Accounts Before Payment (External Debt) ($ millions)		Interest Payment ($ millions)		Debt Servicing	
					% of GNP	Export
	1970	1979	1970	1979	70/79	70/79
Brazil	-704	-7,600	133	2,865	0.9/3.1	12.4/34.6
Egypt	-116	-1,316	38	237	4.1/5.5	28.7/15.8
India	-205	-1,395	189	375	0.9/0.8	20.9/9.5
Indonesia	-286	-1,711	24	722	0.9/4.5	10.7/33.3
Korea, Rep. of	-533	-3,216	70	937	3.1/4.4	19.4/13.5
Mexico	-844	-1,672	216	2,874	2.1/8.8	24.1/64.1
Nigeria	-438	-1,429	30	205	0.7/0.4	4.2/1.5
Pakistan	-591	- 984	76	213	1.9/2.3	8.2/7.9
Singapore	-566	-1,091	6	86	0.6/2.5	0.6/1.3
Turkey	- 28	-7,728	42	253	1.3/1.1	16.3/4.7

SOURCE: *World Development Report, 1981,* August 1981, pp. 158-159.

banks in some LDCs collect all the foreign currency earnings and then dole this out to the appropriately licensed importers to help fulfill the goals of the centrally controlled industrialization plans. Rising populations, increasing incomes and growing industrialization have increased the dependency of LDCs on imports of food, raw materials, and capital goods. Countertrade is one device used to offset the losses of hard currency necessary to pay for imports.[23]

Most LDCs, while not having a system mandating countertrade, have an import-licensing structure that would seemingly encourage such activity. Most imports for hard currency are permitted only under license. Priority is given to capital goods, industrial raw materials, food, and—occasionally—special types of consumer goods. Exporters usually receive favored treatment, that is, a firm that receives hard currency for the exports is more likely to receive favorable treatment of its import request. Generally, licenses are not granted for goods that can be purchased at home. Later in this chapter, policies of specific nations will be discussed in greater detail.

It is important to remember that the developing world constitutes a large and diverse community of countries. Its policies toward importation of goods for hard currency vary significantly. The particular needs of each state are unique. Furthermore, the role that government plays in the economy will vary significantly from socialistic states such as Mozambique and Tanzania to generally free-market systems such as Taiwan and South Korea.

THE USE OF BILATERAL CLEARING ARRANGEMENTS

Much countertrade involving Third World nations falls under the category of fulfillment of bilateral clearing arrangements. Generally, these treaties are between developing countries, though there are also many such agreements between LDCs and countries of the Eastern Bloc. For the nations of the OECD, such agreements are rare. France maintains some special arrangements with its former colonies and Greece has an agreement with Iraq dating from the period before its entry into the Common Market, but generally these bilateral trade treaties are rare.

Usually bilateral clearing account agreements constitute a general statement of goals by two governments rather than a specific contract. A level of desired trade is announced as well as the items that each country wishes to exchange. An account is established utilizing one or more banks, and goods are sent from one country to another with the bank keeping a tally sheet trying to balance the value of the trade. Agreements can be for a single year, or on a long-term basis. Typically, such arrangements are made between countries of the same region. For example, Brazil and Mexico have such treaties with most of the nations of Latin America, Iran with Turkey and Pakistan, India with Sri Lanka and Burma, and so on.[24]

Switch arrangements are sometimes instituted whereby a country with a surplus in its bilateral account and no need for the items offered under the agreement will sell goods at a discount, sometimes for hard currency to a third country or to multinational corporations. Large international trading houses will find the market value for the products by offering discounts to potential customers until they can find someone who wants the surplus items. Such arrangements sometimes undercut the export activities of countries that market similar products utilizing more traditional means of marketing.[25]

WHY LDCs LOOK TO COUNTERTRADE

Because of fluctuating demand for their exports, many LDCs look toward barter as a way to control variations with regard to their import capacity. The hope is to tie or pair imports to exports and thereby maintain stability in their ability to implement industrialization or import large amounts of food.

Multilateral trade on a cash basis involves many factors that are beyond the control of the individual developing country. Nonetheless, a study conducted by the OECD examining the stability of exports of five nations under barter versus a cash-for-goods basis shows mixed results regarding the validity of the claim that barter-like or countertrade arrangements lead to more stable trade. For Egypt and India, exports on a multilateral basis proved more stable. In the case of Ghana, differences were not statistically significant and did not permit the generalization. Tunisia and Sri Lanka, however, showed that for them, barter arrangements had a stabilizing effect on overall trade.[26]

TRADE BETWEEN THE FIRST AND THIRD WORLDS

Trade between OECD countries and LDCs differs significantly from trade between developing countries. First, in trade between OECD countries and LDCs, the hard currency constraint is usually only a factor for the latter party. Second, the OECD country is very often transferring goods, services, or knowledge representing a higher level of technology in exchange for a natural resource or good that is labor intensive.

The likelihood that an LDC will demand countertrade to finance an import will depend on the industrialization strategy of the developing country. For example, a country with a policy of import substitution would be less likely to want to spend hard currency to buy industrial equipment than would one with an export promotion strategy. The licensing policies of most LDCs favor their export industries.

Most governments of LDCs enact laws that will force foreign firms to locate in their countries and then once the firms are established, the LDC imposes export performance criteria, usually in the form of requirements for the percentage of local content that the company must have to qualify for tax benefits or the right to compete for government contracts. Governments of the LDCs will often force foreign multinationals to enter into various cooperative relationships and threaten expropriation if the foreign entity does not conform with its wishes. Once a multinational company opens a plant in a developing country, it is likely to use that factory's production for export to nearby countries. Thus by imposing local content requirements, an LDC's government can stimulate its nation's exports.

The erection of tariffs and strict import licensing criteria are usually the tools by which a government of an LDC encourages a multinational company (MNC) to locate in a developing country. Other inducements such as tax holidays or long-term contracts guaranteeing inexpensive inputs are also common.

Over the last decade, multinational corporations have increased their assembly of industrial products in the developing world. They took advantage of low labor costs, penetrated markets blocked by high tarrifs, reduced costs by locating closer to inputs, and fulfilled the above-mentioned local composition requirements. Nonetheless, the primary sector of multinational activity in the developing world is in the field of mineral extraction. Not surprisingly, countertrade plays a major role.

Large mineral extraction projects frequently require financing of $1 billion or more. Most LDCs lack the ability to finance such operations on their own. As a result, they are not only dependent on Western multinationals for the technologies of exploration, extraction, and processing, but also require Western financing.

Furthermore, the developing countries favor compensation agreements as a way of regulating a fluctuating demand for raw material exports. The LDCs have generally been unable to stabilize their exports of raw materials (zinc, iron ore, bauxite, and copper) and lack the political and economic strength to form a strong cartel. As a result, a long-term compensation agreement holds many attractive features for LDCs.

From the standpoint of the Western multinational, countertrade holds a major advantage over direct foreign investment in raw materials. In the past, a foreign government in the hope of attracting investment would offer almost concessionary terms to companies capable of developing their resources. The mineral extraction industry was and remains not highly competitive so that these governments feel compelled to sign disadvantageous contracts. These agreements are usually of a long-term nature. Once the Western firm establishes production, however, the foreign host government has demanded the renegotiation of the contract. The multinational company is then faced with a dilemma. Having already sunk a lot of money in the project, it could withdraw only with a large loss, so that the firm would usually remain if it could cover its variable costs. As a result of the above risk, the multinationals have tried to move away from holding equity in mining projects and toward "management contracts" or compensation agreements.[27]

Because of the scale of projects in the extraction industry, huge loans are usually required from the governments of the companies and organizations involved. In the United States, the government does not play an active role in facilitating business activity in foreign mineral extraction. Partially as a result, the percentage of American raw material imports from compensation or counterpurchase agreements of the sort described above is not large. For example, a recent United States International Trade Commission study found that roughly 6 to 9 percent of all American imports of raw materials can be attributed to countertrade. The figures for bauxite, copper, chromite, iron, lead, manganese, tin, rutile, and tungsten combined are displayed in Exhibit 3.

Exhibit 3. Estimated U.S. raw material imports ($ millions).

	1974	1975	1976	1977	1978	1979	1980
Countertrade imports*	71	104	107	99	109	109	108
Total imports*	1186	1392	1604	1618	1530	1631	1531

*The study notes that these figures are somewhat understated.
SOURCE: *Analysis of Recent Trends in U.S. Countertrade,* March 1982, p. 22, USITC

Not surprisingly, the level of imports under countertrade, with the exception of 1974, fluctuated far less than the total level of imports. This illustrates why a developing country would prefer a countertrade arrangement rather than a "cash-for-goods" arrangement.

Other industrial countries are far more active in countertrade arrangements for raw materials and strategic metals. Furthermore, in many of these countries, the government helps its country's firms by subsidizing these "develop for import" arrangements through low-cost loans. These activities are often in the form of joint ventures in production. Japan, whose business community and government are most famous for collaboration in planning, is the leader in this field. In 1978, development for import projects accounted for 44.8 percent of Japan's chrome ore imports, 12.7 percent for nickel ore, 10.3 percent for iron ore, and 10.3 percent for copper ore.

An example of such an arrangement is between the Brazilian firm Belem and Japan's Overseas Economic Cooperation Fund, a division of its Import-Export Bank. The Japanese advanced a loan of $800 million and received 49 percent equity in a Brazilian alumina-aluminum complex. To sweeten the deal, this loan was subsidized. Repayment for the loan is in the form of 400,000 tons of alumina and 160,000 tons of aluminum annually.[28]

Many countries of the EEC also partake in similar activities. The French and West German governments subsidize the exploration costs of their countries' firms if the resulting projects will contribute to their raw material imports. The French government picks up 50 percent of the cost of exploration if it occurs in former colonies. The Germans have no similar type of geographical restriction and their government will assume 50 to 75 percent of the cost regardless of the location. Since their national firms not only provide the services for the exploration, but are also likely to receive contracts to provide equipment to establish production, the governments of Western Europe and Japan see such import development policies as highly favorable to their national economies. In this respect, American firms operate at a disadvantage, which is becoming a serious U.S. policy concern.

RECENT DEVELOPMENTS IN COUNTERTRADE POLICIES IN SELECTED LCDs

Countertrade, generally, is an expedient, rather than a desired way of conducting business. Illustrative of this was the situation that occurred in Turkey in early 1978. The Turkish economy in this period was deteriorating. The domestic upheaval contributed to falling exports that were insufficient to finance the country's imports. A large number of American manufacturers either having large receivables or interest in selling their products in Turkey asked the Turkish government through the U.S. government about the possibility of bartering goods in exchange for past due balances or for current exports. The Turkish government's initial response was not favorable. Its foreign trade regime prohibited barter by private firms.[29]

Turkey's balance-of-payments position continued to deteriorate. The situation risked driving American firms out of the Turkish market. In response, the Turkish government reversed itself and permitted the activities of a new company called TURAM Corporation under the sponsorship of two American collection firms, American Bureau of Collections and the U.S. National Association of Credit Management. The scheme was established whereby TURAM would be supplied with Turkish exports, which it would sell abroad for foreign exchange. Creditors would then collect 65 to 75 percent of the selling price against their claims, and the local producer would receive 25 percent of his payment in hard currency. The Central Bank of Turkey would pay the national firm the rest of his price in local currency.

While TURAM was not completely successful in fulfilling its goal, it did obtain convertible foreign exchange for the American firms that required payment. And the use of countertrade as a tool of balance-of-payments crisis management was demonstrated.

Most countertrade agreements involving developing countries are not mandated by law. Instead, they are improvised agreements taking account of the particular needs of the parties to a proposed deal. On January 1, 1982, the government of Indonesia undertook a potentially revolutionary step which may alter the international trade patterns in the direction of increased countertrade.[30] The Indonesian Ministry of Foreign Trade announced a policy of linking government procurements of imports to the exports of Indonesian products, excluding oil and natural gas. The Indonesian government contended that the decline in demand and prices for agricultural and mineral commodities necessitated countertrade obligations.

Over the last few years, Indonesian government expenditures for construction and procurement amounted to $4.5 billion annually. The goods offered for countertrade from the agricultural sector are: rubber, coffee, white pepper, black pepper, tobacco, and manioc; from the industrial sector the products offered are: cement, timber, plywood, other processed woods, and textiles. The amount spent on goods and services in Indonesia in the fulfillment of a government contract will be deducted from the amount needed to be imported by the foreign exporter.

To limit the possibility of widespread dumping of Indonesian goods on the world market, a provision states that "a contractor must undertake to use or resell export goods in the contractor's country of nationality, unless authorization is obtained to use or resell elsewhere." As a result, the likelihood of reexported Indonesian goods competing with Indonesian exports in their traditional markets is reduced.

Failure by the foreign supplier to implement the contract and countertrade for the full value of its export makes the foreign company liable for a penalty of 50 percent of the value of any unfulfilled export undertakings. Thus in contrast to the 10 to 15 percent penalties which are common in contracts with the East Bloc, the Indonesians are far less willing to take their "export" in the form of a further price reduction.

Other developing countries are watching attentively the progress of Indonesia's linkage policy. If Indonesia is successful at attracting foreign firms to sign contracts despite the countertrade requirements, other LDCs may follow suit. Indonesia has one advantage over most Third World states in that ambitious development program sponsored by its government provides many opportunities for foreign firms. A smaller country with less need for foreign imports probably will find foreign companies unwilling to accept its conditions.

The U.S. Department of Commerce is concerned about a possible domino effect of the Indonesian action. It fears that if Indonesia can find companies to deal with, Malaysia, Thailand, Singapore, and others may follow suit. Additionally, the Europeans and Japanese, who are both more willing and more experienced in countertrade, may contribute to the distortion of market prices in international trade. While Indonesia has stipulated that the foreign exporter must dispose of the goods it receives from Indonesia in its home market, it will be difficult to police such a provision in reality.

In Latin America, certain regulations have been instituted giving rise to countertrade. For example, since 1973, Brazil's Industrial Development Council (CDI) has established quality controls for manufacturers. In 1978, a new law, Ordinance 513, was enacted, which establishes minimum requirements for local content of products. These regulations are generally 85 percent. CDI issues certificates verifying the local content that enable firms to bid for government contracts and thereby become eligible for government credit and tax breaks. Any new product that will be produced in Brazil must be presented to CDI so that the requirements for local content can be established. Since many multinational companies use their Brazilian subsidiary for production for the rest of Latin America, a type of countertrade emerges. While companies have the choice to bypass CDI guidelines, the government's role as major or sole buyer in many types of industry, including mining, petroleum, steel, railway, and heavy construction, prevents multinational firms from using its plants only for assembly.

To further increase the local content of finished products assembled domestically, the Brazilian National Development Bank, FINAME, makes available low-cost loans to foreign-owned companies if: (1) there is evidence of free transfer of foreign technology and of technical assistance to the Brazilian subsidiary or joint venture and (2) even higher local content than usual is fulfilled.

Brazil demands a 100 percent local content in the auto industry. Mexico and Argentina presently require 85 percent and 95 percent, respectively. Once the local-content levels had been reached the host governments decided to have the foreign car manufacturers fulfill other national goals. Argentina limited the introduction of new car lines to manufacturers who were exporting Argentinian produced cars. Mexico required that for every dollar spent on imports a firm would have to export an equal amount. Such measures are by no means limited to the automotive industry or geographically to Latin America. The governments of LDCs, however, are not always successful in altering the behavior of the multinational. For example, General Motors withdrew from Peru in 1970, as it did from Pakistan and India when the governments imposed what were viewed as excessive local-content and export requirements.[31]

OIL AND COUNTERTRADE

OPEC's role in establishing the market price for oil has created unique conditions giving rise to countertrade. Members of OPEC are supposed to maintain a common price for their crude oil. If each OPEC country had an identical product, if equal demands existed within each member country for foreign goods, and if there were no substitutes for OPEC oil as an energy source, there would be no problem in maintaining the cartel. These three conditions, however, do not exist. Therefore, the world price for oil is declining in real terms.

Many oil-producing countries are looking to countertrade to finance their ambitious development plans following the decline in real oil prices. States with small populations like Kuwait, United Arab Emirates, and Saudi Arabia can vary their oil sales without producing major social consequences. Such countries as Nigeria, Algeria, Iran, Iraq, and Indonesia have much larger populations, and a decrease in oil revenues, possibly causing a reduction in social spending, might produce dangerous repercussions for the governments in these countries. In response, this latter group of countries has looked for ways to reduce the real cost of their oil so as to maintain or increase their earnings in the face of a falling demand.

Because similar goods received from industrial countries may carry different prices, an oil-exporting country can offer a discount by overpaying for imports while publicly maintaining the official OPEC price. Countertrade deals for oil usually cover a shorter period than do agreements for strategic metals. This is because payment for weapons, drilling equipment, or other goods can be paid for with oil from already existing wells.

The recession in the industrial West and the falling real price of oil have given rise to a number of deals where the oil producer will supply oil over a number of years in exchange for goods. Venezuela's President Luís Herrera refers to the bartering of goods for oil as a part of his concept of "globality." He believes that the current price of oil does not reflect its true value and that Venezuela's reliability as a supplier of oil should be reflected in what it receives for its oil exports. This was first applied under a bilateral clearing arrangement with Brazil where Brazil exported coffee in exchange for oil. Other countries and firms quickly followed suit. The French firm, Elf-Aquitaine, signed a contract to build a refinery in France to process Venezuelan crude and receive payment in oil for its services. Italy and Japan pursued similar deals, providing industrial equipment for crude oil.[32]

While exact data are difficult if not impossible to obtain, the arms-for-oil barter remains one of the primary forms of countertrade. These agreements are very often triangular arrangements. For example, in 1976 Iran provided crude to Shell Oil, which marketed the oil on behalf of BAC, which then delivered aircraft to Iran. A similar arrangement was worked out involving Ashland Oil and General Dynamics, where Iran received F-16s. Countries whose defense industries are government-owned have a distinct advantage in making such deals since they can coordinate their foreign and trade policies.[33]

For the foreseeable future, the conditions which encourage countertrade are likely to continue in the developing world. As more Western companies become familiar with countertrade, the number of such transactions probably will increase. This could have a snowballing effect. As more Western firms conduct countertrade, LDCs will become less hesitant to demand it, thus making the whole phenomenon more widespread. If Indonesia is successful in mandating countertrade with the industrial world, it could signify the beginning of a new era in international commerce.

Appendix

BARTER/COMPENSATION

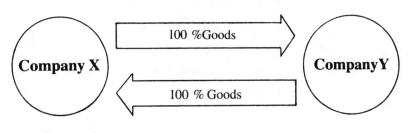

COOPERATION

Industrial Cooperation

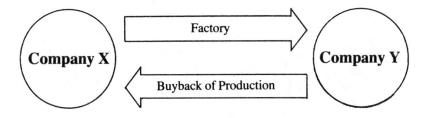

Joint Ventures Without Equity

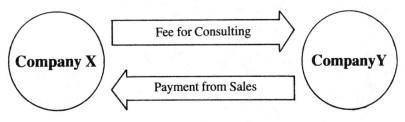

PART COMPENSATION

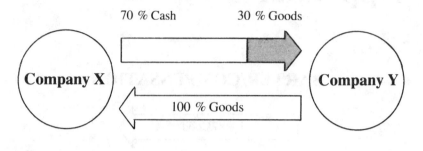

70 % Cash   30 % Goods

Company X   Company Y

100 % Goods

SWITCH
Company X

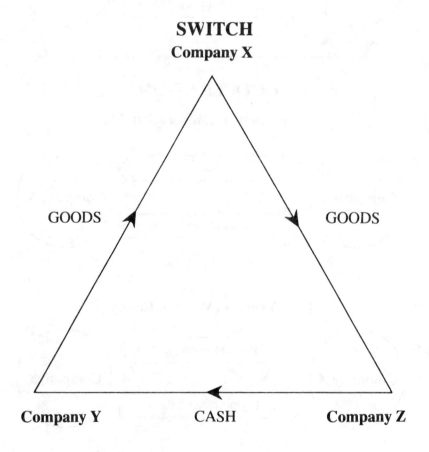

GOODS   GOODS

Company Y   CASH   Company Z

References

1. "Quid Pro Quo," *The Economist,* February 6, 1982, p. 20.
2. Thomas McVey, "The Contract in Barter Transactions," *Soviet, Eastern Europe, China Business and Trade,* and R. F. Baer, *Barter-Countertrade: Basic Legal Considerations,* paper presented before the American Management Associations, April 1, 1981.
3. U.S. Department of Commerce, Pompilio Verzario, *Countertrade Practices in Eastern Europe, The Soviet Union and China: An Introductory Guide to Business,* Washington, D.C., 1980, p. 58 (henceforth referred to as *Business Guide).*
4. U.S. International Trade Commission, *Analysis of Recent Trends in U.S. Countertrade,* Washington, D.C., 1982.
5. "Inside Phillips Brothers: A $9 Billion Supertrader," *Business Week,* September 3, 1979, pp. 108-117.
6. Leo Welt, seminar materials and notes from conference on Business with Eastern Europe, Business International Institute, Vienna, 1981.
7. Hedrick Smith, "Money Problems Plaguing Soviets," *New York Times,* March 14, 1982, pp. 1, 20.
8. OECD, *East-West Trade: Recent Developments in Countertrade,* Paris, 1981, p. 73 (henceforth referred to as *East-West Trade).*
9. *Business Guide,* p. 37.
10. Id., p. 38.
11. *East-West Trade,* p. 74.

12. *Business Guide,* p. 39.
13. *East-West Trade,* p. 74.
14. Id., p. 75.
15. Id., p. 74.
16. U.S. Department of Commerce, "Trading and Investing in Romania," *Overseas Business Report,* Washington, D.C., 1978, pp. 4-8.
17. *East-West Trade,* p. 73.
18. Id., p. 75.
19. Note 7, p. 20.
20. Leo Welt, seminar materials from Countertrade Conference, sponsored by U.S.-Yugoslav Economic Council, March 30, 1982.
21. Steven Marksheid, "Compensation Trade: The Chinese Perspective," *China Business Review,* January-February 1982, pp. 50-51.
22. World Bank, *World Development Report,* 1981, Washington, D.C., 1981, p. 57.
23. Note 4, p. 15.
24. OECD, *The Developmental Impact of Barter in Developing Countries,* Paris, 1970, pp. 30-38.
25. Outers-Jaeger, *Barter-Related Investment Mechanisms,* OECD Development Center, Paris, 1977, p. 3.
26. OECD, Note 24, pp. 85-86.
27. Bergsten, Horst, and Moran, *American Multinational Corporations and National Interests,* The Brookings Institution, Washington, D.C., 1978, pp. 130-133.
28. James Walsh, draft paper, "Develop for Import Policy," 1981, pp. 4-8.
29. Conversations between Leo Welt and U.S. Department of Commerce officials and cables from U.S. Embassy in Turkey.
30. Indonesian Embassy, "Linkage of Government Procurement Policies," January 1, 1981.
31. Note 27, pp. 378-388, and conversations and documents provided by U.S. Department of Commerce.
32. "Venezuela Seeks Goods for Oil," *Journal of Commerce,* April 21, 1981, p. 46.
33. Note 24, pp. 33-44.

Selected Bibliography

African Business and Trade, Welt Publishing, Washington, D.C., 1981-1982

"Algeria Tightens Its Oil Barter Deal," *Business Week,* June 16, 1975, p. 16.

Caves, Richard, unpublished manuscript,"Multinational Enterprises," 1981.

"Countertrade Sales in the German Democratic Republic," *Columbia Journal of World Business,* Spring 1978.

Goldsmith, Carol, "Countertrade Inc." *China Business Review,* January-February 1982.

Lowenstein, Roger, "U.S. Firms Move to Countertrading," *Wall Street Journal,* November 4, 1981, p. 22.

Martin, Everett, "U.S. Firms Are Pressed to Offer Barter Terms by Overseas Customer," *Wall Street Journal,* May 18, 1977, pp. 1, 31.

National Foreign Assessment Center, *Soviet Strategy and Tactics in Economic and Commercial Negotiations with U.S.,* Washington, D.C., 1979.

———, *Handbook of Economic Statistics, 1981,* Washington, D.C., 1981.

Organization for Economic Cooperation and Development, *Countertrade Practice in East-West Trade,* Paris, 1979.

Radez, Richard, "Opportunities in Project Financing," *The Banker,*

August 1978, pp. 54-63.

Soviet Business and Trade, Welt Publishing, Washington, D.C., 1978-1982.

Spetter, Henry, "Countertrade Transactions in East-West Trade: Roles Issue and Limitations," Crossroads, Winter 1979, pp. 221-249.

U.S. Department of Commerce, East-West Countertrade Practices: An Introductory Guide to Business, Washington, 1978.

————, Overseas Business Report, Washington, D.C., 1981-1982 (for selected countries).

"Venezuela May Seek Technical Assistance, Not Just Money in Exchange for Its Oil," Wall Street Journal, May 16, 1981, p. 3.

Weigand, Robert, "Apricots for Ammonia," California Management Journal, Fall 1979, pp. 33-41.

72—